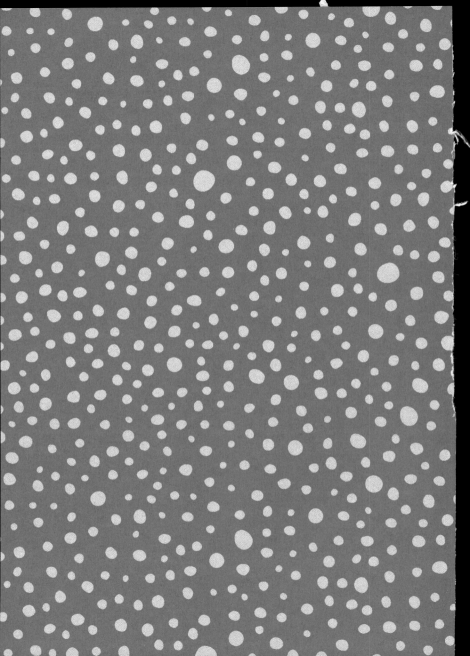

CHAMPAGNE FOR

One

CHAMPAGNE FOR

A CELEBRATION
OF SOLITUDE

REBEKAH ILIFF

ILLUSTRATIONS BY HOLLY MAHER

ISBN: 978-1-951412-40-1
Ebook ISBN: 978-1-951412-67-8
LCCN: 2021911378

Printed using Forest Stewardship Council certified stock
from sustainably managed forests.

Manufactured in China

Design by David Miles

10 9 8 7 6 5 4 3 2 1

The Collective Book Studio®
Oakland, California
www.thecollectivebook.studio

In loving memory of
Katherine A. Rose
Lois M. Holscher
Kathryn M. Iliff

———————

*"The greatest thing in the world is to
know how to belong to oneself."*

— MICHEL DE MONTAIGNE

CONTENTS

———

INTRODUCTION

Ralph Waldo Emerson once said: "Guard well your spare moments. They are like uncut diamonds. Discard them and their value will never be known. Improve them and they will become the brightest gems in a useful life."

The enjoyment of being alone is different from feeling lonely and also distinct from isolation, which is an intentional act of disengaging from an overwhelming world, generally due to fear or force. With active, intentional solitude we recover, we meditate, and we make space for abundance. In essence, we learn to savor our own company; by doing so, our relationships—with ourselves and others—have a shot at striking that increasingly elusive balance.

Finding solitude is surprisingly easy, and we don't need a trip to Italy or an Indian ashram to enact our own version of *Eat, Pray, Love*—although idyllic for soaking up the "spare moments," this is not practical for most. Instead, when we embrace alone time and accept our need for it fully, opportunities manifest themselves everywhere: on a scenic drive down a winding country road, on a meandering stroll in our neighborhood, while having a glass of champagne at our favorite restaurant, or reading a gossip magazine during a bubble bath. When these singular moments are reframed as an individual choice to clutch our "brightest gems," we become powerful participants in our unique, useful lives. Celebrating solitude isn't a luxury; it is an absolute necessity for our personal well-being and the broader world of which we are part.

In *Champagne for One*, I explore the amazing and sometimes awkward aspects of being alone, and how we can behold solitude as a celebration and joyful experience. Whether you are adjusting to single life, happily living alone, newly married, tackling motherhood, or anything in between, I hope to reveal new ways of embracing our need for alone time through personal essays, poetry, satire, and suggested activities—with or without champagne.

Cheers! Prost! Cincin!

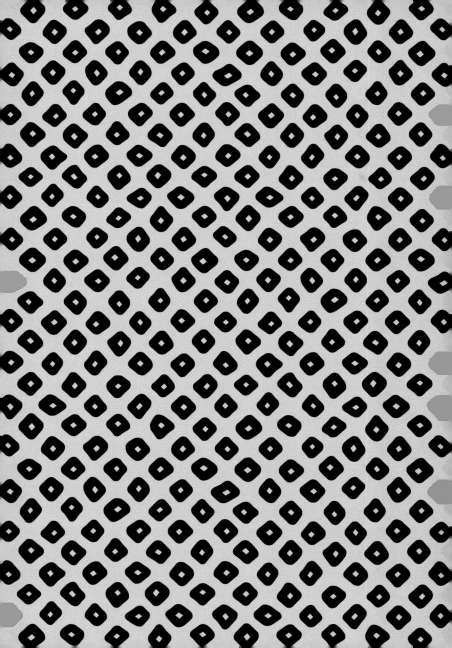

ESSAYS FROM
ONE

IRONIC SOLITUDE

The irony of being alone, even if we are enjoying it, is thinking it would probably be better to *not* be alone. And when we are in moments of aloneness, our mind pulls us into believing there is a 100 percent chance we are missing out on something *extremely* important. This trickery has many faces: the boyfriend who will make us feel loved, a best friend who will remind us of our brilliance and hilarity, and that colleague who flatters us into believing we are irreplaceable. We retract from others to refuel, but an invisible force constantly tugs us from ourselves.

Why is it so hard to embrace solitude for all of its many attributes and life-giving qualities? For starters, modern life has crafted a

> *Why is it so hard to embrace solitude for all of its many attributes and life-giving qualities?*

narrative whereby relationships with others, if not validation from them, is the most necessary element to finding happiness and fulfillment. This is apparent with a simple observation of recent technological innovation: dating apps, social media platforms, and a multitude of communication channels that enable us to connect, even if we have attempted an escape to Antarctica or a Mexican sweat lodge to avoid connecting.

When is the last time you saw an advertisement featuring a young adult sprawled out in front of a fireplace by themselves, perhaps with headphones in, staring off into space, contemplating the wonders of the universe? Or a middle-aged woman sitting at a bar by herself, sipping a glass of bubbly, enjoying a good laugh while she reads an entertaining story? Not lately, right? The message is clear: We must go, we must do, we must achieve, we must constantly relate no matter how superficial. Rinse and repeat.

The myth and hidden message served up with this way of living—leaving little time for contemplation or reflection—is that our personal identity is dependent upon what others think of us, and how we "fit in" to the group. Cultivating healthy relationships with others, who value us and love us unconditionally, is certainly a fundamental aspect of being human; but it's not the whole picture. We may strive for inclusion, but honing our resilience skills when we are left out is likewise paramount.

Much like the stages of grief, fully embracing solitude goes through a similar cycle: Denial tells us we don't need or deserve alone time; or worse, we are losers for wanting or having a lot of it. Then, we become seething and angry at ourselves and those around us as we drown in the cacophony of demands on our time. Next up, we bargain with ourselves and say, "If I do this, then I will prioritize my need for relishing my alone time"—instead of just embracing what is rightfully ours. Soon, dragged down by tasks, to-do lists, and endless time sucks, we fall prey to depression. And finally, once we've hit rock bottom, generally after realizing life is too short to abdicate our own thrones, we accept solitude for what it is: a prerequisite for personal freedom, self-realization, self-care, and being able to live with ourselves. After all, if we don't learn to enjoy our own company, how can anyone else?

Another popular myth the world throws mostly at women, gay or straight, about being alone is that we cannot be complete without a partner. While we have certainly made strides in the home, workplace, and society in terms of "female independence," the mental angst of women, who continually have to explain why they are single or don't have children, sets us back emotionally, socially, and culturally. Instead of being celebrated as stellar bosses, fantastic aunties, integral deputy mothers, and vital big sisters, we often relegate them to one of two corners: commitment-phobes, likely too damaged for any lasting relationship; or, even more insulting, ice queens who are probably unlovable for any variety of reasons—from being too wrapped up in their careers to being entirely selfish individuals. Perhaps truth exists somewhere in there, but, as a general rule, people are complex and life stories are chapters long.

From personal experience, I know the destruction this way of thinking causes. When I look in the rearview mirror and see how many weeks and months (possibly even years) I would get back had I fully lived in acceptance of my alone-ness—my "state of solitude"—it makes me momentarily cringe. Until my mid-thirties, even though I put on a good front of wholly embracing my solitude by traveling alone, showing up to parties alone, and engaging in hobbies alone, I had a nagging feeling that something was wrong with me. I had wonderful friendships, close family relationships, fulfilling professional connections; yet somehow I believed the missing link, the one thing that would surely alleviate all my self-flagellation, was a life partner. Once I shifted my thinking about being alone and, frankly, ignored the endless urgings from well-intentioned people to "freeze my eggs," "perhaps join a convent," or, alternatively, "become part of a throuple," a weight lifted. I quit putting energy into a seemingly futile pursuit. I was open to a romantic relationship, but I wasn't vying for one.

I began to frame solitude as an intentional act of kindness to myself and, by extension, others. From there, things began to shift. Now, husband in tow, I can't seem to get enough of it! And so, the irony is never lost.

SPA·LEBRATION

A bridal party assumed most of the day spa's relaxation area, and they did not disappoint: in true Nashville fashion, they were whooping it up, having exchanged their Broadway boots for oversized bathrobes. Part of me hated them and wanted to direct their attention to several perfectly visible "quiet area" signs throughout the room. The other part of me was nostalgic for memories gone by, when I was the one in the far-too-plush robe romping around with my girlfriends. But today, less than forty-eight hours shy of my thirty-ninth birthday, I was alone and still grieving the recent loss of my best friend, Katie. I knew she would want me to celebrate, to embrace life in whatever form, and so today was my attempt to recapture some joy—if not for myself then at least for her.

While I contemplated my next move—either shushing the bridesmaids or resuming an in-depth *Vanity Fair* profile on Leonardo DiCaprio—the spa attendant approached me, notepad in hand:

"Would you care for a glass of champagne?"

"Absolutely," I said, without hesitation.

She pointed to the only empty chaise lounge in the room, next to me.

"And for your friend?"

Startled by the question, as I had just been thinking about Katie, I looked at the vacated chair, back to her, then back to the chair. I could feel a pair of eyes—presumably the bride herself given the size of the rubber penis atop her head—looking in my direction and awaiting my answer. I wondered if she was expecting another guest and would seize the opportunity to acquire the chaise. *Am I going to be the girl they gossip about later on the Honky Tonk Party Express Bus? The one who ruined their perfectly planned, penis headband–wearing "spa-lebration" with my presence?*

"It's just me," I said at last. I mustered some enthusiasm. "Champagne for one!"

The bride leaned in: "So, you're by yourself and NOT saving that chair for anyone?" Without intention she simultaneously reminded me of my friend's absence and my aloneness—even though I was *clearly* alone on purpose. I felt the urge to pull her toward me by her perfectly luscious waves, grab the faux phallus, and hit her over the head with it. Instead, I forced a smile, and offered a hand gesture that said: *You can have the damn chair.*

Soon enough, I was facedown on the massage table. As the champagne bubbles settled, and I relaxed into the rhythm of hands kneading away at my grief, I decided to cut the bride some slack: Nashville brides—hopped up on booze, hairspray, and nail salon fumes—could not be held accountable for their behavior. I would celebrate my birthday, in all its solitary glory, without thinking of all the ways it could or should be different.

Once the massage was over and I was sufficiently detoxified from the sauna, I returned to the relaxation area, hoping the bridal party was now otherwise engaged. If faced with another encounter, I may be tempted to retract my forgiveness. Thankfully they were nowhere to be seen. The chaise lounge in question from earlier was vacant. I grabbed a fashion magazine from the shelf and claimed the seat, vindicated. The room was completely empty and silent, save the ocean waves soundtrack and buzzing fans, and I was grateful for the solitude at last. The spa attendant entered the room with a tray propped above her shoulder. On it was a glass filled to the brim with champagne.

"Another one for you," she said, walking in my direction. "To celebrate your birthday!"

"How did you know?" I finally said after a pregnant pause.

She winked and carefully placed the glass on the side table. "A little birdie told me."

FRENCH EXIT

n short succession, I learned two surprising facts about France. For starters, when one leaves a fête without saying goodbye, this clandestine act should *not* be referred to as a "French exit," as the term has evolved to mean something of a gross sexual nature. Imagine my brother's surprise when, two hours into a soirée at a New York art gallery, I leaned toward him and whispered: "Shall we make our French exit?" To which he quickly replied, "Sis, I think you mean an Irish goodbye."

I had visited France multiple times, and as his elder was clearly more knowledgeable, so I initially brushed him off. Upon further inspection, I realized he was correct. This subsequently sent my brain into explosive overdrive. *How many times have I softly murmured this into someone's ear at a party, or later bragged about my clever French exit?* Horrified, I admitted to him the error of my ways, and from that point forward opted for the less-offensive Irish goodbye.

The second lesson came by way of a French love interest, who gratefully was not interested in French exits. He did, however, make a point to correct the many inaccuracies related to my Francophilia, the least of which was my frequent misuse of the word *champagne*. According to the Frenchman, using this word "is only appropriate when referring to sparkling wines from the Champagne region of France." Well, *excusez-moi*.

So, if you find yourself on the hunt for the perfect fizzy treat to pair with an evening of binge watching or while enjoying a much needed night out at a swanky bar, here are some rudimentary, yet vital details to know about alcoholic beverages with bubbles:

CHAMPAGNE: As previously mentioned, this libation is the legally defined term for blended "classic method," or *méthode champenoise*, wine making from the Champagne region of France. Different types vary in sweetness levels, from brut to doux, but all are made from Chardonnay, Pinot Gris, and Pinot Meunier grapes.

CAVA: This bubbly goodness hails all the way from Catalonia, Spain. While it uses the exact same method as champagne to arrive at its flavor, it cannot legally claim it, so cava is classed differently. It also has the last laugh because it is priced more affordably than champagne but often tastes just as good (more fruity!), if not better.

PROSECCO: Created by a sassy little method called "Charmat," a two-step process that traps bubbles in wine via carbonation in large steel tanks, prosecco refers to sparkling wine made from the Glera grape in northern Italy. Like its Spanish counterpart, cava, prosecco is traditionally sweeter than champagne.

SEKT: Although slightly late to the fizzy party, the Germans have recently emerged on the global scene with their own reputable sparkling wine. With less alcohol content than most other alcoholic bubbly beverages, Sekt offers a nice option for taking the edge off without completely going over it.

SPARKLING WINE: Often called champagne by mistake by those in much-less-sophisticated countries like the United States of America, sparkling wine is a broad category that refers to carbonated wines of varying types. If it has bubbles, you can technically call it sparkling wine. If you want to knowingly irritate someone from France, call a bottle of *actual* champagne a bottle of sparkling wine.

IN SUMMATION: Champagne is from France. Cava is from Spain. Prosecco is from Italy. Sekt is from Germany. Sparkling wine is a catchall phrase for carbonated wines from anywhere. Bonus: they all pair well *au chocolat*. Drinks with bubbles surely make an evening alone or any celebration worth attending, even if the result is an Irish goodbye in the morning.

BATHROOM OF ONE'S OWN

Conventional wisdom offers all sorts of ingredients for a happy marriage including laughter, patience, friendship, trust, and regularly scheduled date nights. The less touted "personal space" is also a core ingredient, and the lack thereof can throw off even the most heavenly matrimonial bliss. I learned this around age eighteen, when I asked my maternal grandmother how she and my grandfather remained content together after nearly five decades of marriage. With glittery eyes and slightly turned up lips, she said: "Well, honey, he traveled five days a week until retirement."

So before my husband moved into my house—the one I'd proudly purchased and decorated to my liking shortly before our official courtship began—I sat him down for a serious conversation about boundaries. Most gals would likely be concerned with topics such as "What's considered flirting?" and "How many guy trips a year is too many?" Not me. I had only one thing on my mind.

"My love," I said.

"Yes, dear," he said.

"I need to tell you the one seminal rule of this house, now that we're living together."

"Let me guess. You don't intend to start cooking?"

"That's a close second. But no."

"Well, honey, please spit it out. The suspense is killing me."

I took a deep breath, momentarily looked away from his earnest blue-gray eyes, then turned to face him. I put my hand on top of his to show my sincerity and our inextricable connection. I mouthed, "I love you." He tilted his head and smiled curiously. Then he replied: "I love you, too." But the inflection in his voice signaled he was also asking a question. He probably wondered what he was getting himself into. Finally, kindly but with firmness, I spoke.

"Under no circumstances will we share a bathroom."

Before I could gauge his level of confusion (or agreement) with my proclamation, I offered him detailed insight. I explained to him that my bathroom is a sanctuary. It's where I find solitude, say my prayers, and think about what's wrong with my loved ones so I can effectively change them. I can't ruminate fondly about my husband if he is standing right next to me watching me expertly apply my eyebrows. My bathroom is where I ritualistically bathe, conduct my beauty regimen, fuss with my hair, and do things I never want my husband—or anyone else, for that matter—to see or hear. Ever.

How am I to arrive in the bedroom as a desirable object of affection if my significant other has just witnessed an aggressive tooth flossing? And for shame, no one except me with one eye closed is going to get a glimpse of my face as I stare in that torturous magnifying mirror, plucking hairs from my chin. This is surely grounds for divorce.

When I finished my monologue, my husband let out a small sigh and stroked my cheek with his free hand.

"Fine by me, babe. I was actually going to ask if I could have the entire guest suite to myself."

My bathroom is where I find solitude, say my prayers, and think about what's wrong with my loved ones so I can effectively change them.

A SINGULAR POEM

CHAMPAGNE FOR ONE

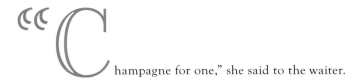

"Champagne for one," she said to the waiter.

"I'll bring a glass for your friend coming later."

"No, no," she replied. "It's just me and this book."
With a look of concern, he pointed to the nook.

"Would you rather sit there, away from the window?"
As if she were an outcast or a grief-stricken widow.

"I'm actually fine to sit right here
among other people, just so we're clear."

With a look of surprise, he set off for her order,
but on his return still showed sympathy toward her.

"Why, thank you, kind sir, for my glass of bubbles
and the compassion you have for my seeming troubles."

But truth be told, she was happy to be
away from the madness and totally free.

So, word to the wise: when you see just one, sit, watch, and learn how it's done.

For being alone can bring great delight
and shouldn't be viewed as some kind of plight.

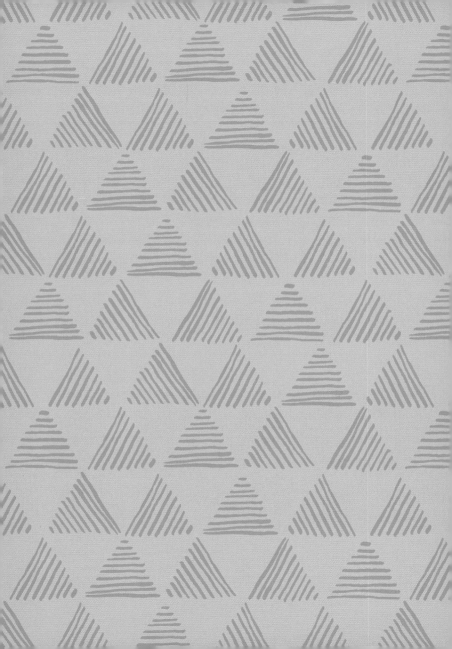

MUSINGS ABOUT
SOLITUDE

LADIES WHO LUNCH

—

October 1, 2018

Dear Penelope,

I'm writing this letter out of concern, and also because when the girls and I drew straws, I got the shortest one. Anyway, the truth is, we are all a little worried about you. To be fair, none of us really know you, but since enrolling your daughter at our school, we've made several attempts to include you in various activities: tennis, lunching, sunbathing, happy hour, lunching, charity-event planning, book club, lunching. Now that I'm writing this, I realize it may seem as though we eat a tremendous amount of food with all that lunching. LOL. Mostly, we just nibble on salad, sip on our favorite Pinot Gris, and catch up on all the latest gossip. I assure you, we are all in tip-top shape! In fact, we go to Pilates AS A GROUP at least twice a week.

Back to my original point, are you telling me that *none* of these activities interests you in the slightest?

Just so you know, we are inviting you because, well, we want you to feel welcome. We authentically care. Moving to a new city, changing jobs, losing your husband in a tragic roller-blading accident, raising a child on your own, purchasing a quaint house, then renovating it—practically all on your own with no interior designer!—can certainly take its toll. Plus, we are always on the lookout for other like-minded, successful women to join our little group!

To see you walking alone everyday along the promenade with your coffee, staring out into nothingness, really hurts us. Almost like we can feel your pain. You must be so sad. Don't you want to make new friends? Don't you want to be involved in the community? We really think it would be best if you found ways to just *move on.* And what better way to do that than to take us up on at least one of our offers to include you? For the record, we don't ask just *any old somebody* along. We believe you are truly special. In fact, perhaps you could consider that a new, personal mantra? *I am truly special.* Mantras are a wonderful way to turn the tide of whatever may be burdening you.

Please consider this yet another invitation (and at this point, probably our last . . . better jump on it!) to join us. On Fridays, we have lunch at the country club from 11 a.m. to 2 p.m. Please swing by, and we can make a toast to you with our favorite Sav Blanc!

Sincerely,

Mia, Charlotte, Meagan (pronounced with a long "e"), Hallie, and Victoria

October 10, 2018

Dear Mia, Charlotte, Meagan (pronounced with a long "e"), Hallie, and Victoria,

Thank you for your generous offer, but I really do prefer champagne.

Truly,

Penelope

SIMON SAYS FOR ALL THE SINGLE LADIES

S imon says, raise your hand if you're a single lady.

Look me in the eyes and call me big daddy.

By George, this is a smart group! Way to go, gals, not one of you fell for the initial test. Let's get on with it then, shall we?

Simon says, stomp your feet like you're crushing all the couples who won't invite you to their dinner parties because they think you will feel awkward. When, in fact, they are the awkward ones.

Simon says, wiggle your hips like you're dancing the night away in an Ibiza nightclub with a sexy Italian billionaire, whilst your married friends stay home and cook dinner, tend to the laundry, and watch paint dry.

Simon says, cover your ears, like you do when that *mean girl* from high school starts yapping about her upcoming nuptials that you aren't invited to attend—because "only people with an actual, legitimate plus-one (not like a casual hookup or your brother who you *always* drag along) are allowed to come, otherwise it will throw off the seating chart. I mean, have you EVER heard of a table for seven?"

Shout "I'm crazy!"

That's it, ladies! I can't trick you for one hot minute. Not only are you NOT crazy, but studies show that the "single at heart" are generally just as happy as those in long-term relationships.

Simon says, fight for your right to participate in broadly known two-or-more-person activities such as: riding roller coasters, eating at a restaurant, going to the movie theater, or playing ping-pong. It's these small wins that will get you one step closer to social acceptance by those who have bought into the "matrimania" ideology.

Simon says, bend over and take it like a champ from the workplace, the marketplace, and the federal tax structure, all of which will screw you at some point for being single.

Slow clap for Beyoncé, whose number-one hit "Single Ladies (Put a Ring on It)" gave you permission to: "Get nice and stanky with me. Where I'm from we do things nice and stanky. We do things nice and funky."

Ha! I nearly got you there. But then, you remembered that Beyoncé was just trying to exploit your vulnerabilities in order to sell records, much like all of those ridiculous, self-help "relationship gurus" who offer a variety of solutions to your singledom—as though it's a problematic plague.

Simon says, applaud for yourself—for withstanding the silly stereotypes created by those afraid of solitude and likely their own shadow.

Simon says, fly like a bird because you're totally and utterly free to do whatever the hell you want.

One last thing: While I'm a huge supporter of each and every one of you, and completely respect your single status, would any of you fancy a drink?

PRAYER FOR SOLITUDE

Our Father, who art in heaven,
hallowed be thy name.
Thy kingdom come (in the form of "me time,"
pretty please),
Thy will be done on earth,
as it is in heaven.

Also, dear Lord, could thy will possibly include:
A weeks-long business trip for my spouse.
My children being abducted by aliens, or angels—whatever is
most pleasing to You.
You can leave Lulu, the dog. If thou wills it.
She is harmless.

Give us this day our daily bread.
And a glass of sparkling wine to celebrate the fact that I made
it through another daily routine.
And forgive us our debts, as we forgive our debtors
except, perhaps, those humans—
You know who they are, Father—
who rob my emotional bank account on a regular basis with

no intention of ever repaying me.

And lead us not into temptation on the Internet,

particularly the colossal black hole of social media.

Deliver us from evil:

Like descending into the fiery pit of *The Real Housewives of Beverly Hills* binge watching,

instead of reading a Pulitzer Prize–winning book by Gwendolyn Brooks or Toni Morrison.

For thine is the kingdom (which I will gladly

visit right now, by myself),

and the power to provide me with sanity,

and the glory that only You can bestow on this solitary soul.

Forever is a REALLY long time, but if You insist, yes.

Yes, I will go to the Hotel Arts Barcelona alone,

no questions asked.

Amen.

*Give us this day
our daily bread.
And a glass of
sparkling wine to
celebrate the fact
that I made it
through another
daily routine.*

SILENT TOASTS

C elebrating life's achievements or marking important milestones alone can feel anticlimactic and even awkward. Whether you've just landed that dream job, turned forty, or kicked a toxic relationship to the curb, recognizing these moments can be a joyous occasion—even when company is scant. If you're open to going solo, then sidle up to your favorite bar in town, or pull up a stool to your in-home bar, and offer a silent toast with your favorite celebratory beverage in hand. Life is simply too short to forgo embracing your breakthroughs and reflecting on life's curveballs.

From spins on old sayings, to original witticisms based on personal experience, here are a few silent toast prompts for almost any solitary occasion:

I acknowledge the hard work it's taken to reach this landmark occasion, and I accept that I am kind of a BIG DEAL. Scratch that. I'm a REALLY BIG DEAL. Cheers!

To the bliss of being single, the fun of seeing double, and the comfort of sleeping triple.

Roses are red,
violets are definitely not blue.
I raise this glass to me
and definitely not to you.

From this day forward, in celebration of this occasion, I will do my best to be who my dog thinks I am.

Lots of fancy business people say you can't manage what you can't measure—but I can't seem to manage shit right now, which probably means I'm not measuring up. However, at this very moment I'm managing to have a measured moment of peace and quiet with a very tasty beverage in hand, and that is simply enough for now. Salut!

May the force continue to be with me. (Head bow.)

With these bubbles, I do spread . . .
Good cheer and feelings of joy to all those around me . . .

*Life is simply
too short to forgo
embracing your
breakthroughs
and reflecting on
life's curveballs.*

Particularly the super-hot bartender, who seems to think I ordered the bottomless mimosa. But who am I to complain? Cincin!

May I live as long as I like,
and have all I like as long as I live.

I have known myself for a very long time, and I am so grateful to still be able to tolerate myself, in spite of myself. This alone is a major accomplishment. Thus, my hat goes off to myself for making it through one more year with my dignity intact. I raise this glass to myself, by myself!

I moved the needle for your business.
Then you moved me out of the business.
But now I have my own successful business, and I'm eating your business for breakfast, lunch, and dinner. So, who is moving now? Take that, suckers.

Sometimes one must climb a giant mountain over and over and over again. Thank God I am still here to tell the story. Hallelujah. Amen!

Four bottles for one of us,
thank God I can take the bus!

Today, I put my past in the past. Now, my next chapter begins. I pray that it will be at least slightly better than the last—although I have much to be grateful for, including good hair. Namaste.

As I continue to slide down the pesky banister of life, may the splinters refrain from pointing in the wrong direction.

Ok, well, this feels weird, but here goes nothing:
I F***ING KILLED IT!

SOLITUDE FAQS, ANSWERED BY A THERAPIST

QUESTION: Why does craving alone time make me feel guilty?

ANSWER: That's a wonderful question. There could be a variety of reasons. But you definitely shouldn't feel guilty—unless of course you're neglecting your duties. Are you? Even then, guilt is questionable.

QUESTION: How do I know if I'm feeling lonely versus embracing my alone time?

ANSWER: Oh, you'll know.

QUESTION: What is the best way to tell others I need a break?

ANSWER: Kindly, but firmly.

QUESTION: What if I require alone time every day?

ANSWER: What if you do? Let's explore.

QUESTION: How much time alone is too much?

ANSWER: It really depends on you. How much time do *you* think is too much?

QUESTION: If I'm in a room filled with people (let's say a yoga class), but it's pretty much silent, does this count as solitude?

ANSWER: Quite possibly. How are you feeling in the moment?

QUESTION: I really enjoy my solitude. Does this mean I'm "single at heart" and will be a terrible failure in a relationship?

ANSWER: It's a probability, but hard to say for sure.

*Do I need to go to
a meditation retreat
in a distant country
to find solitude?*

QUESTION: Do I need to go to a meditation retreat in a distant country and forgo all first-world conveniences—like endless supplies of fizzy water and groceries-on-demand—to find solitude?

ANSWER: Do you?

QUESTION: What if my partner thinks it's weird that I need to be alone much of the time?

ANSWER: If your partner thinks it's weird, they are likely projecting their feelings of weirdness about something entirely unrelated to your need to be alone.

QUESTION: Is it strange that I don't enjoy parties with large groups of people, and I would rather stay at home alone binge-watching Shonda Rhimes's latest creation—dog at feet, glass in hand?

ANSWER: We are all strange in our own, unique ways. Perhaps I could interest you in journaling?

QUESTION: If I'm in the car with my kids, and I secretly want to leave them by the side of the road to fend for themselves while I sneak off to a hotel and spend three nights by myself, does this mean I'm overdue for some alone time?

ANSWER: Please remember, I am under legal obligation to report any potentially harmful behavior to yourself and others. But between you and me, off the record, I had this very same thought last week.

QUESTION: Does the fact that I'm asking so many questions about being alone mean I'm probably overthinking this whole solitude thing?

ANSWER: To that, I can most definitely answer, "Yes."

CONVERSATION ENDERS

When I was nineteen, I frequently traveled home to Topeka, Kansas, from Chicago to visit my family. On these trips, I made a point to spend alone time with my baby brother, who is nearly twelve years my junior. We would jump into our mother's minivan—I in the driver's seat, while he insistently parked himself in the last row. At the time, he was small for his age and continually reminded me that "it isn't safe for me to sit in the front seat quite yet." So, instead of sitting within earshot, where we could have an audible conversation, he headed to the farthest recesses of the vehicle. Clearly not taking the hint, I would shout at him from the front seat, asking him all sorts of questions about school, friends, activities, our parents' recent divorce, and his current favorite color, animal, book, and time of day. No topic was off-limits.

He was a very polite, well-spoken, yet contemplative child who, even at a young age, willfully traded aimless chitchat for a walk inside his own head. On one of these outings, he'd clearly had enough of my interrogation and said abruptly, "Can you please stop talking so I can think?" Coming from a seven-year-old, this was both insulting and hilarious at once. But I understood where he was coming from and immediately granted him silence. After a few minutes of being alone with his own thoughts, he came to life. He proceeded to tell me, in great detail, about a series of "dragon books" he was writing. I learned a vital lesson about the beauty of silence and listening.

Contrary to popular belief, like my baby brother, you may not be interested in striking up conversations with random strangers *or* people you know, even if they are. While all sorts of tips for *starting conversations* invade our news feeds, business advice columns, and personal development sections at bookstores, it's perfectly normal for you to wonder: "But what if I want to END a conversation?"

Of course, you can always attempt to avoid eye contact, feign a phone call, throw on your earbuds, or invent a convoluted story about the imminent death of your pet hamster to signal you are not "open for business." However, speaking from my own experience of being oblivious to silence signals (read: he headed to the farthest recesses of the vehicle), some people are simply terrible at taking hints.

If you ever find yourself in need of a solid shutdown, here are a few suggestions for creatively inspired *conversation enders* that may just do the trick.

IF YOU'RE AT A BAR OR RESTAURANT

I just received a phone call from my doctor (technically she's a dentist), and it appears I've contracted some bizarre gum disease that easily jumps from person to person. Would you like to try a sip of my cava?

―――――――――

Let's see: first kiss? Oh yes, age five. The family dog, Rufus. Never had better.

―――――――――

Will you excuse me for one moment while I relieve myself? My goodness, nine times in one hour must be some type of record! Must have been all that cheese . . .

―――――――――

Correct. I am the founder of a dog rescue. Yes, the dog rescue is in my home, and I have forty-eight special-needs dogs, some of which are incontinent, living with me in a 450-square-foot apartment. They all sleep in my twin bed.

―――――――――

Actually, my boyfriend, <insert fake name>, is a world-class MMA fighter. He's always up for a bit of competition . . . if you are?

―――――――――

IF YOU'RE STANDING IN LINE

And to think, by this time next week the doctors say I'll be dead!

Do you ever get this overwhelming desire to trip an elderly person as they're crossing the street? Sometimes, I even feel the urge—that is, if they are in a wheelchair taking up the ENTIRE sidewalk—to push them into a grassy knoll nearby, where they will most certainly get stuck. Maybe it's just me?

Pardon me. I don't speak <whatever language they are speaking>.

Why yes, I agree the weather is lovely, and I too am looking forward to the big game this weekend. However, I'd really rather talk about politics, if you don't mind.

The real question is: do you prefer doing drugs immediately upon waking up, after lunch, or during supper?

I only use my gun when absolutely necessary. Would you like to see it?

IF YOU'RE ON AN AIRPLANE OR ANYWHERE EQUALLY INESCAPABLE

I don't mean to be rude, but I'm just *dying* to listen to this podcast. I've been meaning to *knock it out* for weeks. Nothing better than understanding the inner workings of a *serial killer's brain*. Amirite?

Would you rather unplug from the Internet for an entire year and live in a cave *or* jump headfirst off a bridge with no bungee cord into a burning California forest fire *or* meet your end in a fiery plane crash?

Je ne sais pas.

I *only* use my gun when absolutely necessary. Would you like to see it?

My favorite time of day is around 2 a.m., when I wake up from my mid-morning nap, withdraw myself from bed (well, it's more of a coffin), and wander aimlessly around my house searching for bats. You?

I recently finished reading the most amazing book about the Yugoslav Wars. Shall I recite it to you from memory? It all began in 1991, when constituent republics declared independence, despite unresolved tensions between ethnic minorities in the new countries. This subsequently fueled the wars . . .

LAST WORD

If none of the above result in the desired effect, and your neighbor continues to babble on about their impending bunion removal surgery, perhaps the best approach for ending a conversation comes from my brother: Can you please stop talking so I can think?

PLAYING SOLO

RECIPE FOR STAG STEW

D elightfully robust with a kick of naughty, this easy-to-follow recipe will have you reveling in your alone time faster than you can say "beat it." Buyer beware: overindulgence may leave you feeling supercharged and without certain "friends" lurking around, feeding on your precious energy.

> *4 ounces confidence*
> *6 ounces "letting that shit go"*
> *¾ cup embracing personal freedom*
> *¾ cup not caring about other people's opinions*
> *1 cup good humor*
> *1½ cups books, magazines, and shows you love*
> *1 gallon of your favorite fizzy beverage*

Blend confidence, "letting that shit go," personal freedom, and not caring about other people's opinions in a giant bowl until smooth. Slowly mix in good humor, books, magazines, and shows you love. Top it off with your favorite fizzy beverage. Garnish with a snorting laugh. If you're feeling super saucy, throw in a dab of ignoring your family obligations and a pinch of giving the middle finger to your annoying neighbor.

Serves one.

SOLITARY REFINEMENT

I f we wait for the perfect time to leave our kids with a babysitter, put down our task lists, or break away from work obligations, we will *never* find the opportunity. But refining our spare moments can turn into refueling adventures with a little creativity and simple planning. We don't have to go far to clutch our brightest gems, and if you're up for flying solo, do it with intention—and, if possible, your favorite sparkling wine.

THE MOVIES . . .

Where else can you hide in the dark, binge on buttery popcorn, shove candy in your face, drink your choice of "bad for you" beverage, *and* be entertained without lifting a finger? Traditionally thought of as an activity for two or more, going to the movies alone is a signal of confidence and self-care . . . not to mention a "who cares?" attitude. Because, frankly, who *does* care? The same can be said for going solo to the theater, the symphony, or a concert showcasing your favorite crooner.

Champagne for one? Yes, definitely. Simply smuggle a split and straw inside your purse and sip away.

A MUSEUM OR GALLERY . . .

Big cities have no dearth of museums, art or otherwise, to peruse on rainy days. Most regional cities have at least one museum and a handful of galleries. The point is, it's easy to find something that encourages meandering and daydreaming while using the time to unwind and perhaps even gain inspiration. As an added bonus, an onsite or nearby cafe is a fantastic place to pick up a treat (beverage or otherwise), and museum gift shops can provide much needed "retail therapy" after you're through.

Champagne for one? Absolutely, but likely afterward at the museum cafe or your restaurant or bar of choice.

THE LIBRARY . . .

Whether you're bookish or not, libraries suck you in and replenish the soul. They are quiet and perfectly positioned for solitude as you wander through the stacks, and all that wisdom in one place has an inexplicable, magical component. Grab a book or bring your own, then find a cozy corner to disappear in for as long as you possibly can. Bonus: generally speaking, libraries prefer phones on silent—so you don't have to worry about inadvertently eavesdropping on needless chatter about someone's upcoming dinner party or the ball of wax they've recently removed from their ear.

Champagne for one? It depends. If you can find a nook away from the main desk, chances are no one will notice you taking swigs from your "water bottle."

A LONG DRIVE . . .

Escaping for an hour on a drive to nowhere is often a quick fix for finding solitude. Alone in a car, winding through country roads or a city you love (avoid highways, they seem to have the adverse effect) is accessible to minivan-driving moms, carpooling dads, and single sisters alike. While you obviously have to pay attention and can't completely tune out (unlike an art museum), creative juices and new energy get moving while you listen to your favorite tunes or preferred podcast. If weather permits, let the windows and your hair down.

Champagne for one? Certainly not while driving, but save it on ice in a cooler, then enjoy it after your journey.

THE BATHROOM . . .

Bathrooms are so much more than meets the eye. A toilet can double as a chair, a vanity as a mini-bar, and the bathtub as a makeshift chaise lounge. If you're surrounded by people—small or sizable, loved or loathed—you can head to the nearest bathroom for some solitude. Hide without guilt, knowing if something really did go south, you could easily reappear within seconds. Make sure to keep an extra stash of gossip magazines (and maybe even a Bible for really challenging days) along with your favorite beverages under the sink. If you need more convincing, see "Bathroom of One's Own" (page 29).

Champagne for one? Of course!

A MINDFUL WALK . . .

It may seem simple, but walking is often the antidote to feeling lousy or overwhelmed. Paradoxically, embarking on a walk alone often makes us feel *less* alone, because "far from the madding crowd" we gain perspective. The endorphins give rise to positive emotions, and all the negative things we may be feeling—about a break up, a loved one's death, or an unintended "reply all" email revealing your true opinions about a client—have the time and space to process.

Champagne for one? This one largely depends on how co-ordinated you are in terms of doing things while walking. Perhaps consider a fizzy beverage afterward?

BOUTIQUE BROWSING . . .

Perusing your favorite local boutique or retail shop on your own can reinvigorate the spirit. Finding solitude among things that bring you joy is the perfect way to recharge. Shoes, flowers, lingerie, soap, home goods, luxury furniture, outdoor gear, sportswear . . . it's a greenfield opportunity for chucking your worries and reconnecting with yourself. Buyer beware: this particular activity may get expensive, but window shopping is equally acceptable.

Champagne for one? Probably not while shopping, but definitely when you're through.

A SWANKY HOTEL BAR . . .

What a lovely place to enjoy your own company, dress like you mean it, and people watch as unsuspecting hotel guests become your subjects of study. Besides, why should couples on date night or best friends catching up get all the fun that a plush, designer bar offers? Bring a magazine or a good book to offset any awkwardness, and put that phone away so you can fully soak up the scene. P.S. This is where those conversation enders may be useful (page 79).

Champagne for one? Absolutely. 🥂

PLAYLISTS FOR ONE

I n her essay "The Goal of My Writing," Ayn Rand fa-
mously claims: "Art is the technology of the soul."
Furthermore, "art does not teach—it shows, it displays
the concretized reality of the final goal." Above all other art
forms, music—particularly lyrics and melodies that give us
joy, a space to contemplate, and time to refuel—encapsulates
her sentiment most obviously, if not profoundly.

Music is an integral part of the human experience; and
when we are alone, whether by choice or by force, we often
find comfort in its companionship. When we hear music that
resonates with our soul, we suddenly feel free to envision who
we ought to be, and we simultaneously know the truth about
who we dare not become: automatons whose lives consist of
refrains others find interesting or acceptable, rather than
a collection of individual notes we've chosen for our own,
crowning hymn.

Our life *is* art.

Perhaps you have a playlist you listen to regularly, one
that puts you in a good headspace. Or, maybe you could use
some inspiration to get you started. Either way, as the grand
finale for this book's "champagne for one" theme, below are

a few suggestions for tunes whose final goal is to *show* us the beauty, tragedy, comedy, and necessity of solitude in an endlessly active world.

- "In My Own Little Corner"—LaVerne Butler, *Love Lost and Found Again*
- "Hymns to the Silence"—Van Morrison, *Hymns to the Silence*
- "The Introvert Song"—Peter Mayer, *Elements*
- "Wildewoman"—Lucius, *Wildewoman*
- "Solitude Is Bliss"—Tame Impala, *Innerspeaker*
- "Me, Myself, and I"—Beyoncé, *Dangerously in Love*
- "Here I Go Again"—Whitesnake, *Saints & Sinners*
- "In My Room"—The Beach Boys, *Surfer Girl*
- "Here"—Alessia Cara, *Know-It-All*
- "Perfectly Lonely"—John Mayer, *Battle Studies*
- "Solitude Island"—Calm Shores, *Fall of a Raindrop*
- "I Am a Rock"—Simon & Garfunkel, *Sounds of Silence*
- "On My Own"—Samantha Barks, *Les Miserables*
- "Where I Find God"—Larry Fleet, *Where I Find God* 🍾

FINAL WORD: THE ART OF SOLITUDE

———

Exhausted by another day on the battlefield, balancing motherhood and career, Laura carried her boisterous toddler to the playroom and situated her amidst a sea of stuffed animals. When she turned to leave, Annabelle was confused: "Where are you going, Mommy? Stay with me and play!"

Barely keeping it together, Laura replied: "Annabelle, Mommy needs some alone time."

Upset by the denial of a playmate, her daughter screamed through stilted tears. "Why don't you want to play with me? Who likes to be ALONE anyway?"

Now over the edge and on the verge of her own tears, Laura spun around to face her daughter: "I DO!"

Momentarily startled to silence by this exploding retort, Annabelle's bright blue eyes blinked rapidly, crying ceased; she turned to a teddy bear for solace as Laura quickly descended the stairs and locked herself in the master bedroom.

Refueled after several minutes of complete silence, a few deep breaths, and a hot shower, Laura climbed the staircase and appeared in the playroom just as Annabelle finished a tea party with her prized collection of dolls—each one in various stages of disarray. Upon hearing her mother's footsteps, she spun around, and a grin appeared. "Mama! Come play!"

This time, Laura obliged.

Years later, we still laugh about this story. Not only because one of my best friends since childhood and a known introvert somehow created a child who is her polar opposite, but because it is timelessly relatable and objectively universal. We have all been in situations where someone—a child, spouse, friend, parent, sibling, co-worker, or complete stranger—wants something from us that we simply cannot give.

While locking ourselves in the bedroom may not always be an option, training ourselves to pursue recovery time vis-à-vis solitude *is* always available. Whether we perfect the Irish goodbye, develop our own conversation enders, schedule in time for mindful walks in nature, or routinely enjoy champagne alone at our favorite restaurant, confidently retracting from the demands on our time affords us, as Emerson pointed out, a chance to clutch our "brightest gems." By ignoring pleas from others to join the ceaseless noise, we embrace spare moments to reveal the diamonds in our one and only useful lives.

ACKNOWLEDGMENTS

Thank you, reader, for purchasing this little book: a project born from a big, sweeping grief that brought me to my knees. Through my recovery process I found The Second City, built a supportive writing cohort, and discovered laughter's power to heal. Broadly speaking, I am grateful for all of my independent-minded friends and family members who refuse to take heat for their wild and sometimes crazy choices, and who push through the incessant noise to find their own joy. I want to acknowledge the creative work of the Collective Book Studio along with my thoughtful editor, Amy Treadwell, and talented illustrator, Holly Maher. To my loving husband and accidental muse: thank you for accepting me for who I am—even though I never let you come into my bathroom and won't speak to you for the first thirty minutes of the day. For my lifelong friends and cousins, I continue to grow in gratitude as the years pass on, because nothing compares to the relationships you made during the bad-hair, brace-face, bra-stuffing years. To my adulthood-acquired friends, thank you for the investments you continue to make despite the pulls of everyday life to prioritize other things. Lastly, thank you to the places in Nashville where I find reflection and life-giving solitude: Percy Warner Park, Pure Sweat + Float Studio, Nashville Yoga Co., John P. Holt Library, Belle Meade Historic Site and Winery, and Westminster Presbyterian Church.